Butterfly BASICS

MATTHEW OMOJOLA

OCTAVE PHOTOGRAPHERS, LLC
PHOTO BOOKS FOR CURIOUS CHILDREN

Published by Octave Photographers, LLC

www.OctavePhotographers.com

PREVIOUS EDITION PUBLISHED UNDER THE TITLE:
Morayo's First Book of Butterflies

FIRST EDITION, *Butterfly Basics*, 2020

Hardcover ISBN: 978-1-953588-01-2
Paperback ISBN: 978-1-953588-02-9
Mobi ISBN: 978-1-953588-03-6
Library of Congress Control Number: 2020916114
Cataloging in Publication data on file with the Publisher.

All photographs are from the personal collections of the author.

Camera and Lens information:
Canon EOS 6D and iPhone XS Max
Lens: Canon Zoom Lens EF24-105MM 1:4 L IS USM

Production: Concierge Publishing Services

Printed in the United States of America
10 9 8 7 6 5 4 3 2

To Naomi Morayo
the leader of the
new generation

This is Blue Morpho butterfly with its wings folded. It looks like the Common Buckeye butterfly. It has brown, white, and yellow patterns. It has large eyespots on the folded wings. It has four legs resting on a green leaf. It is found in Canada, United States, and Central America.

This is Zebra Longwing butterfly with wings wide open. It has several alternating white and black bands like the Zebra. It is feeding on a red flower. It is found in Central and South America, Southern United States, and the Caribbean states.

This is a feeding station for the butterflies. Adult butterflies don't eat their foods; they suck their foods! Their mouth is a long tube named proboscis. They like to suck water on leaves and puddles to get minerals from the soil, and juice from fruits and rotten animals for other nutrients.

This is Malachite butterfly. It is folding its wings behind its back. It has brown, yellow, white, and lemon green colors. It is standing on its four legs on a green leaf. It can be found in Central and South America.

The long club-like black structure on its head is the antenna. The brown circle under its antennae is the eye. They have big eyes so they can hunt for food, and keep an eye out for predators.

This is the Rusty-tipped Page butterfly. It is white, brown, orange, and black in color. It is almost completely brown when it folds its wings. It is found in Southern United States and Central and South America.

This is the Emperor Swallowtail butterfly. It is one of the most beautiful butterflies in the world. It has two tails and two eyespots on its lower wings. It is the largest butterfly in South Africa. It can be found in South and East Africa.

This is the Blue Wave or Tropical Blue Wave butterfly. It has blue wavy bands on its black wings. It has many white patches on the fringe of its wings. Butterflies usually have two antennae, and they use them for smell and balance. This butterfly is usually found in the rain forest of South America.

This is the Common Lime butterfly. It is also called lime or lemon butterfly. It is also a swallowtail butterfly. It is one of the most beautiful butterflies in the world. It has six legs, and it is feeding on a pink flower. Notice his big black eye. It can have up to 17,000 tiny lenses in one eye! (You only have one!) The Lime butterfly could be found in Asia and Australia.

This is the Rice paper or Paper kite butterfly. It is mostly white with black lines and yellow patches. Its wings are practically see-through! It is resting on its four legs. It is found mostly in South East Asia.

This is the Blue Clipper butterfly resting on green leaves. The clipper is a very powerful butterfly and flies very fast. Butterflies generally have four wings, two in the front and two at the back. The Clipper is found in the rain forests of Africa and South East Asia.

This is the Monarch butterfly. It is one of the most common butterflies in North America. The Monarch is also called the common tiger, the Wanderer or Milkweed. It spends its winter in Mexico.

This butterfly was the first one to go to space.

This is a Cairns Birdwing butterfly. Its wings are large like those of a bird. It is beautiful. This Birdwing butterfly has six legs and a large yellow abdomen or belly. The circle in front of its face is the "proboscis."

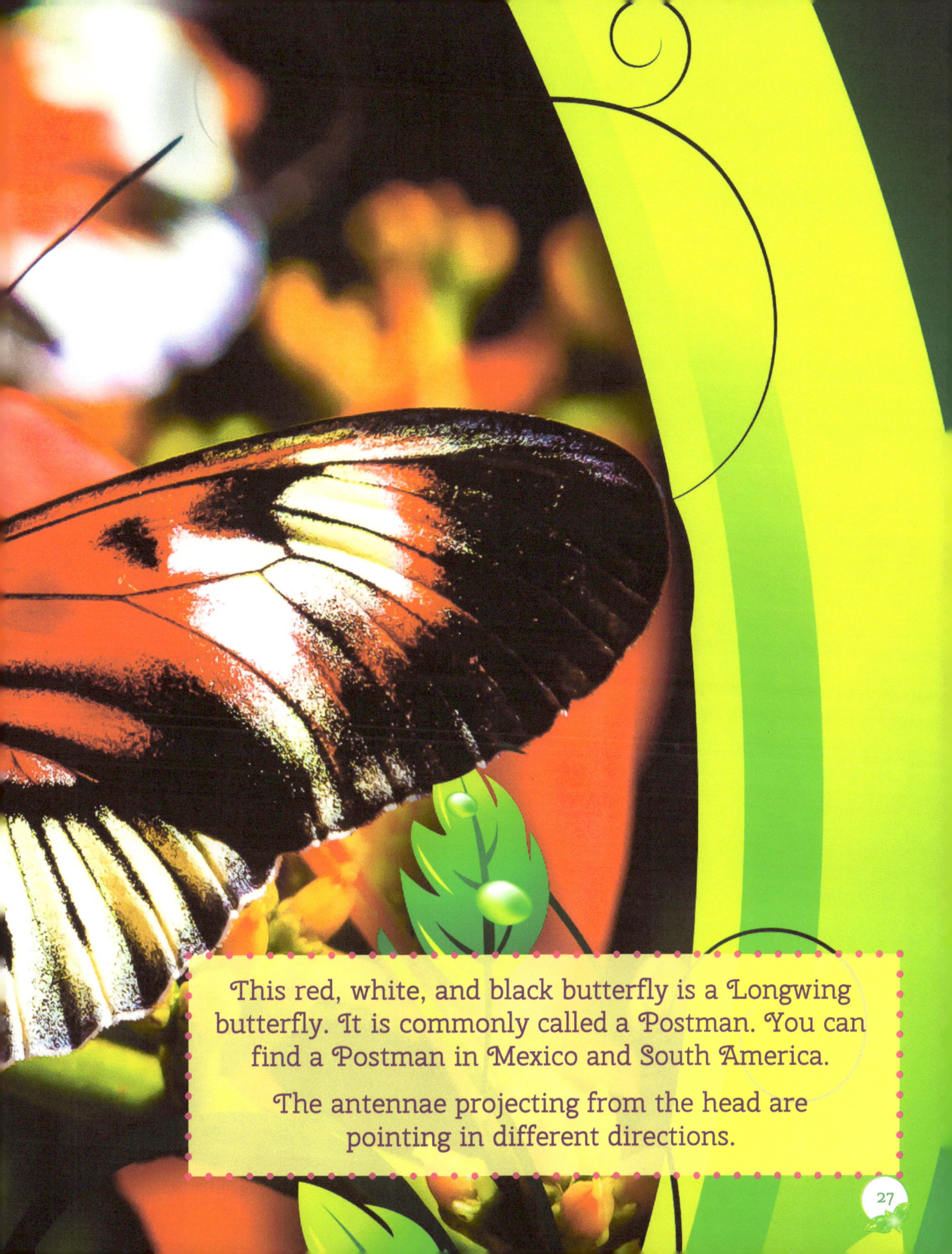

This red, white, and black butterfly is a Longwing butterfly. It is commonly called a Postman. You can find a Postman in Mexico and South America.

The antennae projecting from the head are pointing in different directions.

This large white and red butterfly is also a Longwing butterfly. It has very long wings. It is also called a Postman. Notice the black lines going through its wings. Those are veins carrying blood to all areas of the wing. Butterfly bodies have three parts: The head, the thorax (chest), and the abdomen.

Books in this series:

Butterfly Basics

Butterfly Buddies

Butterfly Masks

Butterfly Funny Names

To order the other titles
in the series, visit:

www.OctavePhotographers.com

and Amazon.com or
your favorite bookstore

Dear Reader,
The author loves butterflies, and photography. Butterflies
are beautiful and graceful, each with their own colors and
shapes. The author and the publisher do not guarantee
the accuracy of the information in this book. This book is
solely for the entertainment of children.
Please enjoy this book!

www.ingramcontent.com/pod-product-compliance
Lightning Source LLC
Chambersburg PA
CBHW060854270326
41934CB00002B/137